CRAIG FOSTER & ROSS FRYLINCK

A JOURNEY UNDER the SEA

CLARION BOOKS
An Imprint of HarperCollinsPublishers

Come visit one of the most magical places on earth. Float up to the clouds and let them carry you south. Fly high over snowy mountains and misty green jungles. And when at last the land meets the ocean, you will have arrived. You will be at the tip of South Africa, where we all began.

Dive into the clear, cold water and you will find yourself in a forest of liquid light. You can relax and explore—the sea holds you safe in a salty embrace.

Below the surface, the seaforest
is alive with curious creatures!

In a whirl of bubbles, a friendly seal pup arrives. He was born on a nearby island and has grown strong on his mother's warm milk. Now he is on an adventure to find food all on his own. *Come on,* the pup seems to say, *swim deeper and see what adventures you can find.*

This shy rockfish is so small, she can fit into the palm of your hand. Let her know she is safe, and you can play a game of hide-and-seek for a while.

Swimming farther along reveals more surprises . . . what's this? Come closer, but ever so slowly, so you don't scare her away. An ocean magician is trying to hide by gathering fronds to cover her face.

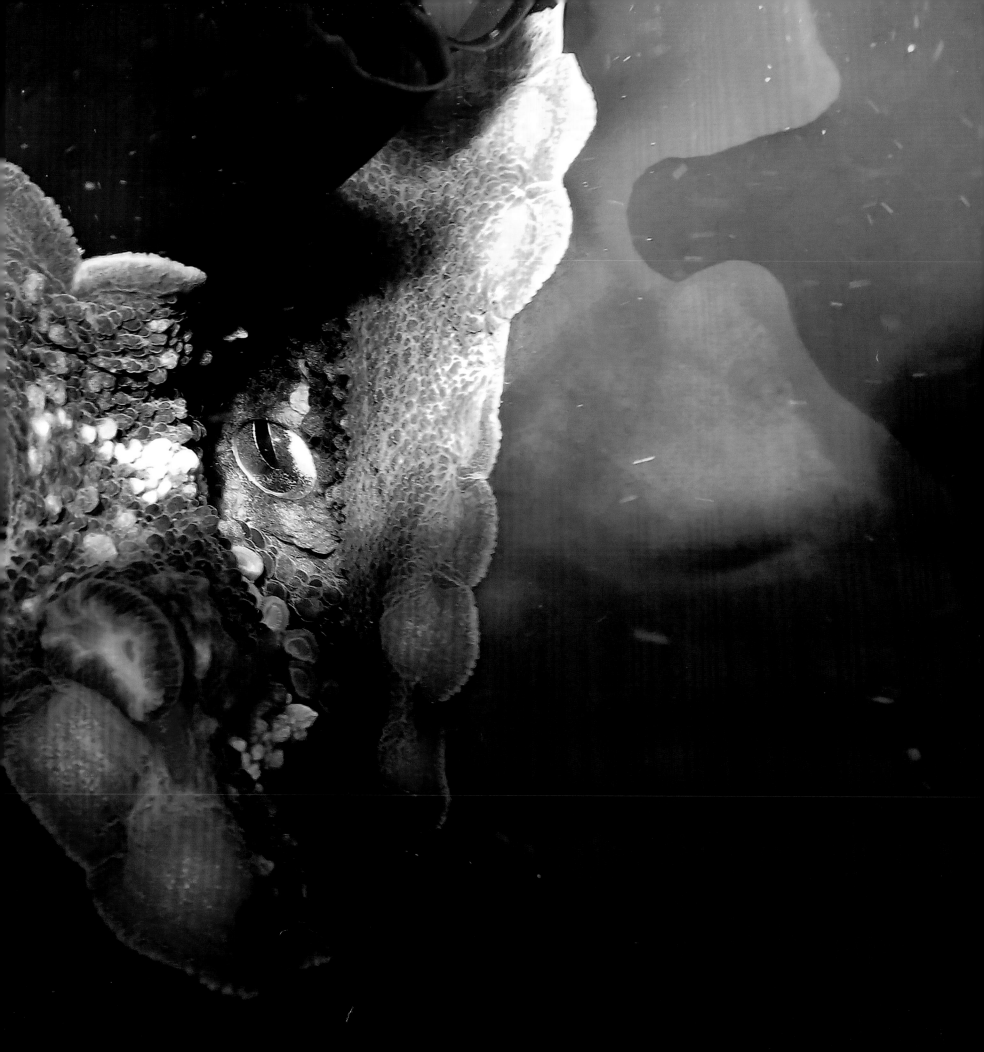

And now she has wrapped herself in an armor of shells and stones! The clever creature is using tools to protect herself.

Suddenly, a swirling cloud of black ink appears. The sea turns dark, and when it clears, the creature has vanished. With her inky powers and magical skin that can change color and shape, it's hard to tell where she is. Will you ever be able to find her?

In a flash, she slips off her brilliant disguise. Here she is, revealed in all her splendor—it's the wonderful shape-shifting octopus! She waves her arms and shimmers and twinkles her skin before she is off on her way once again.

Before very long, a new visitor arrives. It's the octopus's cousin, a shy little cuttlefish. He swims like a jet and is another great master of disguise.

The cuttlefish stays very still.
See how he hides by pretending
to be a whelk shell—can you

Actually, it seems like *everyone* in the seaforest is hiding . . . but from what?

Slowly, a great hunter swims past. Cow sharks
are older than the dinosaurs and have made
their home in these waters for 400 million years.

If you peer under the nearby rocks, you'll find a little cave where a pyjama shark family sleeps through the day. These small hunters can be fierce, but they are very shy around humans.

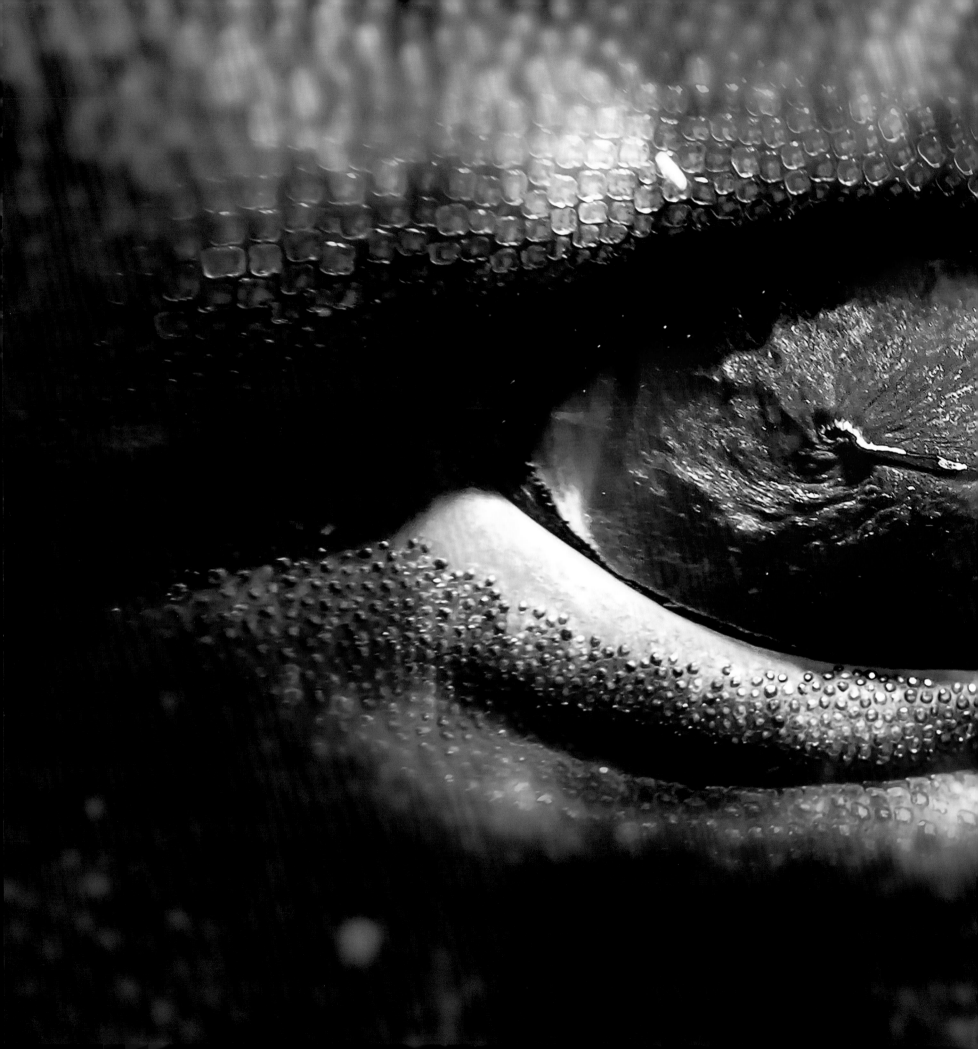

If one wakes up, look into his eye. Stare awhile and maybe you will see an alien galaxy blazing in the deepest reaches of space. The shark won't stay awake long, so enjoy the view and then let him dream on.

What's that yellow spaghetti doing so close to the sharks' cave?

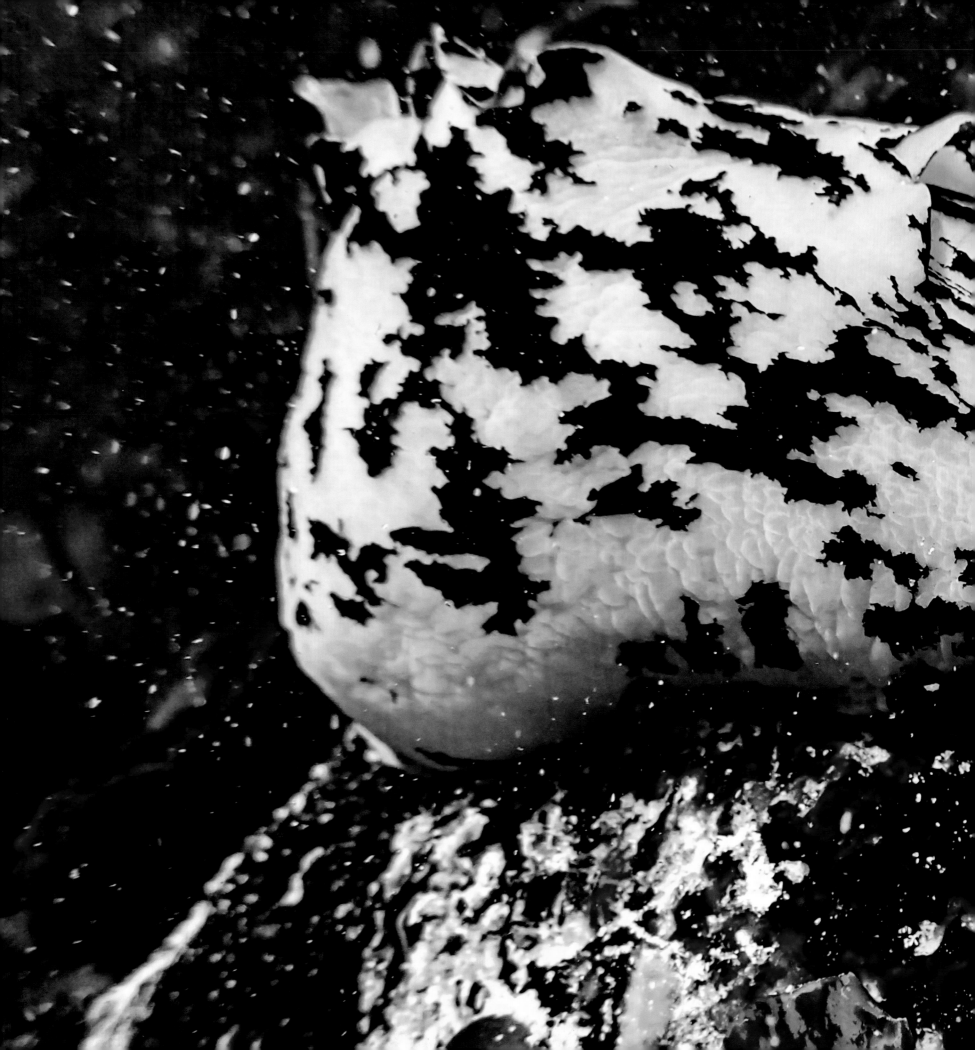

These thousands of eggs belong to the green mother sea hare. She is squidgy and soft, but she's poisonous if eaten and is luckily safe from the sharks.

It's almost time to start swimming back up from the deep . . . but before you go, millions of tiny helmet snail eggs drift past. While they may be some of the smallest creatures of the sea, each little snail might one day become part of the biggest of whales!

Part of a whale—how can this be? Well, you are what you eat, and these sea snails are a tasty whale snack. All the creatures of the sea are connected, and the big needs the small to make up an ocean.

It's getting late, and your journey under the sea must soon end. Luckily, the dolphins have come to guide you back home. Remember the wild, hold it safe in your heart, and return anytime the wind and the waves whisper your name.

A NOTE FROM THE AUTHORS

We grew up by the ocean at the tip of Africa. Our houses were so close to the sea, we could hear the whales singing on windless summer nights. We started to dive when we were very young, and the Great African Seaforest was our underwater home, our magical kingdom. Her animals were our wild kin and our childhood inspiration.

We call this place where we live "the heart of the world," because this is where our species (*Homo sapiens*) began, in Southern Africa. This is our original human home.

As adults, we spend every day visiting our magical childhood kingdom, but now we study the secret lives of wild animals in a deeper way. By following tiny clues and marks in the seaforest, we have slowly learned to track and understand the wild language that these animals "speak." This is not a language of words, but a language of the wild. It is the oldest language on earth, and something our ancient ancestors knew well.

Through this practice, we've discovered a world that is even more fantastical than our greatest childhood dreams and fictions. But the strangest thing of all is that this world is totally real.

Each day, we see the wild animals thrive, and in that cold and enchanted underwater forest we find a great sense of joy and peace. Despite the intense pressures on our planet, this wild African place at the edge of the earth gives us hope.

It's our joy to share a slice of this wonderful world with you. May you get a chance to enjoy being in the water soon.

Foster

RM Frylinck

Archaeological and genetic studies point to Southern Africa as being the most likely place for the origin of our species, *Homo sapiens*. It's quite likely that the ancestor of every human that ever lived walked this wild African shore.

Diving without a wetsuit in Atlantic seawater makes us feel alive and healthy because our brains release feel-good chemicals induced by the cold (average temperatures in the Great African Seaforest range from about 51 to 62 degrees Fahrenheit [11 to 17 degrees Celsius]). The stress from the cold stimulates our immune systems and contributes greatly to a healthy body and mind.

Ranging in shape, size, and color, there are 24 species of klipvis—or rockfish—in South Africa. The super klipvis is the most inquisitive and will follow divers and approach very close. They also follow octopuses, hoping for scraps when they attack prey.

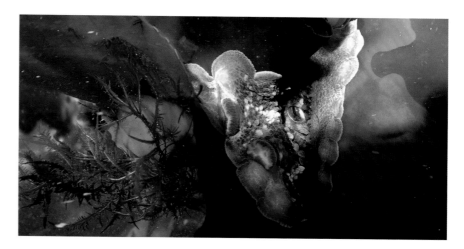

This octopus is using the kelp fronds to create a shield to protect herself from a predator. She does this by holding the slippery kelp with her suckers and wrapping the fronds around her soft body. Octopuses live fast and die young, with most species reaching only about 1.5 years. But their keen intellect and ability to produce thousands of eggs make them very resilient creatures.

These red roman fish live in groups in the kelp forest. They hunt small octopus, cuttlefish, and other invertebrates. They are all born female and when the single male dies, the largest female will change into a male to take his place.

Cape fur seals live on islands and wild shores. They hunt for fish and invertebrates in the ocean. Males grow up to 770 pounds (350 kilograms) and can even kill large sharks, while females reach 330 pounds (150 kilograms). They have two layers of fur and a layer of blubber to keep warm in the cold water.

This octopus has gathered shells from the seafloor to create a hard armor for protection. During evolution, the octopus lost its shell to favor a liquid-like body capable of pouring through the tiniest crack (a handy escape trick). Now the clever creature has learned to make a temporary shell!

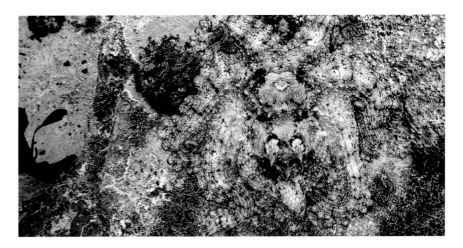

Octopuses have learned to fool the predatory fish eye through ingenious camouflage. They can quickly match colors and brightness by adjusting tiny sacs of color pigment in their skin. They can also rapidly change texture by lifting tiny muscles under their skin into different shapes.

This octopus is displaying a form of what's called "dymantic" posture. This is a type of body language that says, *I'm big, I'm bright and dangerous, so stay away from me.* She does this by extending and curling her telescopic arms and opening the webbed skin between her limbs.

This cephalopod is a tuberculate cuttlefish, found only in South Africa. He uses jet propulsion to swim by pumping water through his flexible siphon, allowing the cuttlefish to swim backwards, forward, or sideways. Cuttlefish have eight arms and two attack tentacles. Octopuses only have eight arms, no tentacles.

These ancient sevengill cow sharks grow up to 10 feet (3 meters) in length. They sometimes hunt in packs to bring down large seals, dolphins, and even other sharks. They have very long tails that propel them at great speed, then they glide like stealth bombers toward prey, keeping their bodies still. However, they are mostly gentle around humans as we are not seen as a food source.

Pyjama sharks grow only to three feet (1 meter) in length. They don't need to continually swim like larger sharks to keep oxygen flowing over their gills. Instead, they do what's called "buccal pumping," which allows them to breathe and sleep together in caves. They can reach 35 years of age and reproduce by laying two eggs at a time. Because they mature late in life, grow slowly, and have few young, they are a very vulnerable species.

The cuttlefish on the right is changing shape, color, and texture to mimic the hard-shelled whelk on the left. He is even mimicking the tiny white polychaete worms growing on the whelk shell. A visual predator like a fish will see "hard shell" and not attack this soft-bodied cuttlefish.

The Great African Seaforest is our underwater home. In rare moments of grace, we feel the "forest mind"—the deep biological intelligence that resides in this wonderland—whispering to us. This species of large kelp, *Ecklonia maxima*, grows up to 45 feet (14 meters) in length. The kelp sequesters carbon, helping to mitigate climate change, absorbs toxins, and protects coastlines from erosion by dampening swell.

While pyjama sharks' dominant sense is smell, they can see 10 times better than humans in low light. This is because the sharks' bodies are able to extract the mineral aragonite from seawater, which builds layers of crystal to form a kind of light-absorbing mirror inside their eyes.

Sea hares are very camouflaged and look just like the algae they eat. So we use their brightly colored eggs to track and locate them. When we see the eggs, we know the adult sea hares are close by.

This is a green color morph of the usually brown variable sea hare. These animals are very slow and would seem vulnerable to predation. However, they are extremely toxic, so predators leave them alone. They have short life spans and only live for about a year.

Helmet snails emerge from under the sand to lay great towers filled with thousands of eggs. These eggs hatch to become veligers, tiny swimming mollusks. Later in life, the veligers change into tiny snails with shells and sink down to the seafloor.

It's rare to see a humpback whale in the kelp forest. They come in to feed on the crustaceans and small fish. It's very exciting to watch them power down with huge tail thrusts and open their gaping mouths to take in thousands of tiny animals in one gulp.

Dolphins have such good hearing that they can survive and still catch fast-moving fish even if they become blind. They do this using echolocation, sending out sounds that bounce off objects, which are received as an echo in their lower jaw. In this way, much like bats, they see with sound. This is very useful for hunting in murky water, and for avoiding predators.

For my son Tom—when I look at the ocean through his eyes, I'm filled with hope. —C.F.

This one's for you, Joseph—keep surfing, keep smiling, forever young and free. —R.F.

SEA
CHANGE®
PROJECT

*Sea Change is a community of scientists, storytellers, journalists, and filmmakers who tell stories
that connect people to the ocean, motivating them to help regenerate our living planet.*

HarperCollins book printing paper is sourced from mills whose forest management practices are certified by
independent, internationally recognized sustainable forestry certification bodies such as Forest Stewardship Council
(FSC), Programme for the Endorsement of Forest Certification (PEFC), Sustainable Forest Initiative (SFI) and
Canadian Standards Association (CSA). Suppliers who source wood from third party suppliers must provide proof that
wood supplied by their third-party sources has been harvested in an environmentally sound manner.

Clarion Books is an imprint of HarperCollins Publishers.

A Journey Under the Sea
Text copyright © 2022 by Craig Foster and Ross Frylinck
Photographs copyright © Craig Foster except for: Pippa Ehrlich: p. 6/7; Tom Foster: p. 4/5;
Ross Frylinck: pp. 8/9, 40/41, 49; Faine Loubser: p. 38/39.

ISBN 978-0-35-867786-4

Typography by Cara Llewellyn

22 23 24 25 26 RTLO 10 9 8 7 6 5 4 3 2 1

First Edition